Praise for other bo

"Chris Morphew is like Tim Keller for teens. In the *Big Questions* series, he tackles some of today's tough questions with Scripture, wisdom and clarity—and just the right amount of fun to keep young readers turning the page. I cannot wait to put these books into the hands of my three children."

CHAMP THORNTON, Author, *The Radical Book for Kids* and *Why Do We Say Good Night?*

"Chris spends his days around young people, and you can tell—his writing is readable, biblical and full of stories."

ED DREW, Director, Faith in Kids

"Our biggest questions prepare our hearts to hear God's greatest answers. Pick up Chris Morphew's Big Questions books and find key gospel responses to your kid's honest questions about God and his plan."

BARBARA REAOCH, Former Director, Children's Division, Bible Study Fellowship; Author, *A Jesus Easter* and *A Jesus Christmas*

"*Why Does God Let Bad Things Happen?* addresses the tough topic of God's goodness in a world of great suffering, and it does it in a winsome, easy-to-read way. Yes, it's for young people, but I'm recommending it to people of all ages—and I commend this remarkable book to you!"

JONI EARECKSON TADA, Joni and Friends International Disability Center

"*Who Am I and Why Do I Matter?* takes one of the core truths of Scripture and explains it in a way that middle-schoolers (and their parents) can understand. I can't wait to put this into my children's hands, and also encourage them to put it into the hands of their unbelieving friends."

JOHN PERRITT, Director of Resources, Reformed Youth Ministries; Author, *Insecure: Fighting Our Lesser Fears with a Greater One*; Host, Local Youth Worker Podcast; father of five

"Chris is the teacher you wish you had. He gets where you're coming from and takes your questions—and you—seriously."

DR NATASHA MOORE, Research Fellow, Centre for Public Christianity

"What an excellent series—seriously excellent! I am certain Chris Morphew's chatty style, clear explanations, relevant illustrations and personal insights will engage, inform and equip tweens as they work through some of the big questions they and their peers will be asking."

TAMAR POLLARD, Families Minister, Wahroonga Anglican Church, Sydney, Australia

"Reading a Chris Morphew book is like sitting with a friend, with an open Bible between you, asking all the tough questions that are on your heart and getting solid, straight, honest answers that line up with God's word—answers that bring you to the light and hope and truth of Jesus. I love friends like that!"

COLIN BUCHANAN, Singer/Songwriter

HOW CAN I BE SURE —WHAT'S— RIGHT AND WRONG?

CHRIS MORPHEW

Illustrated by Emma Randall

thegoodbook
COMPANY

To Cathy Tucker,
Thanks for everything!

How Can I Be Sure What's Right and Wrong?
© Chris Morphew 2023.

Published by:
The Good Book Company

thegoodbook.com | thegoodbook.co.uk
thegoodbook.com.au | thegoodbook.co.nz | thegoodbook.co.in

ISBN: 9781784988715 | JOB-007262 | Printed in the UK

Illustrated by Emma Randall | Design by André Parker

Contents

Chapter 1

CAN WE EVER REALLY KNOW WHAT'S RIGHT AND WRONG?

"Yeah, I hear what you're saying," my friend shrugged, leaning aside as a waiter came by to top up our water glasses. "I just don't see why you need to bring God into it."

I stuck a forkful of pasta into my mouth, buying myself a bit of thinking time, wondering how in the world we'd got here. Five minutes ago, we'd been having a perfectly normal conversation about our plans for the summer break, and now all of a sudden we were talking about the meaning of life—about what it means to be a good person.

"Well," I said, finally swallowing, "I guess, for me, the whole way I figure out what right and wrong even *are* is by looking at Jesus."

"And that's great if that works for you," my friend said, "but you know I don't believe in any of that stuff. And you still think I'm a good person, right?"

"Well, I mean, obviously I don't think following Jesus means I'm a better person than you are," I said. "But that's kind of my point: if there's no God—if we're all just here by accident—then who decides what a 'good person' even is?"

"Don't *we* decide that?" my friend asked. "Anyway, it's really not that complicated, is it? Think of it this way—" He leaned in towards me, gesturing with his fork. "Let's say you found out tomorrow that God didn't exist."

"How would that work, exactly?"

"I dunno. Say they uncover Jesus' tomb and it turns out his bones are still in there. But, whatever—somehow you become convinced there's no God. Would it honestly make that much difference to the way you lived?"

"Of course it would!"

"*Would* it, though? Would you stop loving the people around you? Would you run outside and start murdering and stealing, just because there was no God to say you shouldn't?"

"Well, for your sake, I hope not, but—"

"Exactly." He poked his fork at me again. "My point is, you're absolutely welcome to your beliefs, but I don't need God to tell me what's right or wrong, and neither do you. Seems to me like we've both got it covered already. I mean, when you get right down to it, isn't it mostly just common sense?"

□□□□□□□□□□

The title on the front of this book is, "How can I be sure what's right and wrong?" Figuring out the answer matters because most of us want to be, on balance, good people who make good choices—and we want to live in a world with other good people who make good choices too.

There's a lot I could say about that conversation with my friend, but I tell you this story because I think it paints a picture of the way most people in our culture make sense of morality—of what's right and wrong:

Sure, we all have different beliefs about the world, different ways of figuring out what's right, but don't they mostly come out to the same place?

Be kind rather than cruel.

Be honest rather than dishonest.

Do what you can to make the world a better place.

Treat other people the way you'd like them to treat you.

We might disagree on some of the details, but when you get right down to it, isn't basic morality pretty simple? Don't we all just kind of *know* what's right and wrong?

On the surface, that all sounds pretty reasonable. Basic right and wrong seem straightforward, at least in theory. But you don't have to look very far before things start to get a lot more complicated.

□□□□□□□□□□

Think about it: If right and wrong really are so obvious, then why is it that politicians can never stop arguing about the best way to run the country? Why do people spend so much time debating with total strangers on the internet? Why are so many families and friendships torn apart by drama and disagreement?

If morality is so simple, why all the fighting?

Well, there are probably a bunch of reasons. But I think at least part of the answer is that, sure, it might be simple enough to agree on a few basic *ideas* about morality—but as soon as you start trying to bring those ideas into the real world, that agreement starts to break down.

Figuring out *that* we should be kind to other people is the easy part.

Figuring out *how* we should be kind to other people is a whole lot harder.

□□□□□□□□□□

Let's say you have a friend who starts making some choices you *really* disagree with—choices you're convinced are going to land them in a world of pain and trouble.

What's the kindest thing to do?

Should you keep out of it and respect their freedom to live

how they want to live? Or should you try to talk to them about it? Should you try to convince them that *your* ideas about what's right and wrong in this situation are better and clearer than *their* ideas about what's right and wrong?

And if you do decide to talk to them, what if they don't listen? Is it more loving to honour their choices, or to step in and try to change the situation?

Is there even really one right thing to do here? Or are there multiple different decisions that would all be equally "right"?

Meanwhile, even when you *do* think you've figured out the right thing to do, what if it turns out you don't actually *want* to do what's right? Or what if you *do* want to, but you're scared of the consequences?

It's complicated, right?

And the same thing is true when you zoom out to bigger, more global questions. It's easy enough to agree that people should aim to create a better world. What's way harder to agree on is what that "better world" should actually *look* like, and what steps we should take to get there.

Spend five minutes scrolling online and you'll find all kinds of people with all kinds of opinions about everything from climate change to racism to education to refugees to mental health to who the next president or prime minister should be.

And so if we agree that we want a better world, but we can't see eye to eye on what it is or how to get it... how much are we actually agreeing, after all?

Meanwhile, with so many different opinions out there about right and wrong and how to make the world a better place, you might start to wonder: in the end, is that what all this morality stuff really comes down to? Is it all just opinion?

Or are some things *actually* right and other things *actually* wrong, no matter what we say about them?

□ □ □ □ □ □ □ □ □ □

Ok. So it's complicated.

But still, why bring God into it?

(Because, not to give away the ending, but I do plan to bring God into it.)

Maybe you're on the same page as my friend, back at the restaurant. Maybe you're not convinced that God even exists—and even if he (or she or it) does, why would you need their help to figure out how to live your life?

Or maybe, to you, God seems worse than just irrelevant. Maybe you look at some of the ways religious people behave, or some of the ideas about right and wrong that the Bible seems to teach, and think it seems like the complete *opposite* of a good and moral life. Maybe bringing

God into this conversation doesn't just seem pointless; maybe it even seems harmful.

Or maybe you've grown up in a family that loves and follows God, and you've heard all along that he's our good and loving King, and so of *course* he's the one who gets to say what's right and wrong. And so far, you might've just assumed that was true—but now you're starting to wonder if it actually checks out. Is God's vision of right and wrong really the only way, or even the best way, to live? What about all the people you know who leave God out of the picture and still seem like good, decent, moral people?

These are the kinds of questions we're going to spend the rest of this book exploring, but here's the short version:

The reason that, despite all those questions, I'm *still* determined to bring God into it—and, more specifically, the God I believe Jesus came to show us—is that I'm convinced he can help us out here in ways that no one else can. I'm convinced that Jesus invites us into the truest, clearest, most life-giving way not only to *understand* right and wrong but to actually start living that reality out in our everyday lives.

But, like I said, there are plenty of other opinions out there. So before we get to God, let's start by taking a look at some of the *other* ways people try to figure out what's right and wrong.

Chapter 2

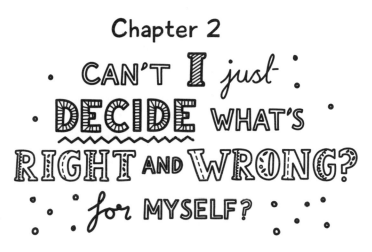

CAN'T I just DECIDE WHAT'S RIGHT AND WRONG? for MYSELF?

Let's take a step back. Because, ok, maybe agreeing on what's right and wrong is more complicated than it sounds—but if that's true, then isn't there a really simple solution to that problem?

Can't we just agree to disagree?

The world is full of all kinds of people with all kinds of opinions about right and wrong, about what's best for the world, about the best ways to live your life.

So why not just let everyone *have* those opinions?

Why can't everyone just decide for themselves what's right and wrong?

You live however seems best to you, I'll live however seems best to me, and we'll all just kind of figure it out.

Sounds pretty reasonable, right?

I mean, what gives anyone else the right to tell you how you should be living your life? Shouldn't each of us be free to make our own decisions about this stuff?

As long as we all respect each other's point of view—as long as you don't try to convince me that *your* opinions about what's right and wrong should be *my* opinions about what's right and wrong—shouldn't we all be able to get along?

□ □ □ □ □ □ □ □ □ □

Here's what's really true and helpful about this way of looking at things:

You are going to spend your *entire life* running into people who think differently to you about what's right and wrong. Even if you manage to surround yourself with family and friends who mostly agree with you, the internet is an endless firehose of other people's opinions, and so if you can't figure out a way to be ok with people disagreeing with you, you're going to have a pretty miserable life.

On the other hand, the more you take the time to understand other people's opinions, and the more respectful you are towards people who think differently to you, the easier it's going to be for you to get along in society.

The world is a diverse place—and what this "figure out your own right and wrong" idea is trying to do (at it's best, anyway) is give us all a solid way to hold onto that diversity and still get along with each other.

ㅁㅁㅁㅁㅁㅁㅁㅁㅁ

What's also true is that there are plenty of situations where agreeing to disagree really isn't a big deal. There are plenty of choices we make in life that aren't moral choices. These choices aren't about good versus evil; they're just matters of opinion.

For example, I know some people who have *extremely* strong opinions about whether or not pineapple belongs on a pizza—but when they argue about those opinions, they're really just talking about which option they prefer.

A person who thinks putting pineapple on pizza is a terrible idea isn't claiming that you're evil if you do it; they're not saying you should be locked up in prison for your crimes (or if they are, they have some very intense views about pineapple).

They might feel really strongly about their perspective; they might have all kinds of convincing reasons to explain why they think their opinion makes the most sense.

They might argue that the juice from the pineapple makes the pizza crust soggy.

They might pull in an expert and tell you that celebrity chef Gordon Ramsey agrees with them that putting pineapple on pizza is a bad idea.

They might just say that pineapple and cheese don't mix.

But in the end, hopefully, all they're really saying is, "I prefer my pizza without pineapple on it".

You might agree or disagree. You might feel strongly that someone who disagrees with you is making a worse *choice*—but hopefully you don't think they're a worse *person* for making that choice.

Most of us would agree that "Does pineapple belong on pizza?" isn't a question about right or wrong, good or evil; it's just a question about our opinions.

ㅁㅁㅁㅁㅁㅁㅁㅁㅁㅁ

But what happens when we pick a more serious example?

In Ancient Rome, the oldest living male in a household was known as the *paterfamilias*—the father of the family. Whenever a new baby was born into the family, the child would be placed on the ground and the *paterfamilias* would be brought in to take a look. If he decided he wanted to keep the child, the father would pick up the baby and raise them into the air, officially welcoming them into the family.

On the other hand, the father might decide *not* to pick up the baby. Maybe the child had been born with a disability; maybe the child was a girl when he'd wanted a boy; or maybe the father just decided he didn't want another mouth to feed. Whatever the reason, if the father decided he didn't want the baby, he'd just leave him or her there on the ground. He'd turn away from the baby, and then someone else from the household would take the child outside and abandon them on the street to die of hunger, thirst, cold, or animal attack—or to be snatched up by a stranger and sold into slavery.

This practice was known as "exposure", and it was just a normal part of Ancient Roman life. Sure, a few people back then argued that it shouldn't happen—that every newborn baby deserved to be loved and cared for—but mostly, people just kind of went with it. They didn't see it as evil; they saw it as the father's right to do what he wanted with the children born into his household.

So, what do you think? Should we bring this back? Should we start doing it again?

I'm really hoping that idea is just as unthinkable to you as it is to me.

It's all well and good to agree to disagree about pineapple on pizza, but when it comes to something like *this*, the situation changes, right?

If you found out today that dads were ordering that their babies be left outside by the trash cans, I'm guessing you wouldn't just shrug your shoulders and say, "Well, everyone should be free to live however seems best to them".

I'm guessing there's something deep in your bones telling you that abandoning a newborn baby to die on the street is truly and deeply *wrong*.

ooooooooooo

And this brings us to maybe the biggest problem with the idea that everyone should get to decide what's right and wrong for themselves: it might sound like a really generous, open-minded, inclusive way to live—but no one really believes it all the way through.

There are plenty of things we're happy to agree to disagree about, and in a society full of different opinions, that can be a really helpful attitude.

But the truth is, we all draw the line somewhere.

We all have *some* things where we think there's only one right answer, where we think everyone should agree with us, where we say, "I don't care what anyone else says, that's just *wrong*".

ooooooooooo

Ok. But what if someone actually goes all the way?

Imagine a person who says, "No, I mean it: everyone should be free to decide what's right and wrong for themselves about absolutely everything—even abandoning helpless newborn babies!"

Even *that* person isn't following their own advice. In fact, just by making that statement, they're *already* demanding that people agree with *them* about what's right and wrong.

Think about it: when you tell people that everyone should be free to decide what's right and wrong for themselves, what are you *really* saying? You're saying it's *right* to let people decide what's right and wrong for themselves— and you're saying it's *wrong* to stop them from deciding for themselves.

We can't escape it. One way or another, we all draw the line somewhere. Which means that using "agree to disagree" as our solid way to get along with each other turns out not to be so solid after all.

However it is that we're going to figure out what's right and wrong, we need something better than each person just deciding for themselves.

Chapter 3

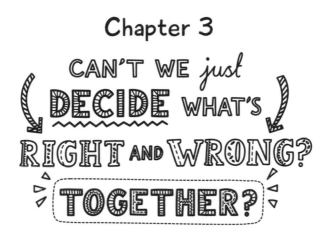

CAN'T WE *just* DECIDE WHAT'S RIGHT AND WRONG? TOGETHER?

O k. So if agreeing to disagree can only get us so far—if we can't just decide for ourselves what's right and wrong—then what about the next logical option?

What if morality is something we decide *together*?

A world where everyone just does whatever they want all the time is obviously going to fall apart pretty quickly, but what if we work together and come to some sort of group decision about what's right and wrong?

Clearly, this won't be *easy* (because, like I've said, the world is full of all kinds of people with all kinds of opinions about this stuff)—but is it *possible*?

Can we all come together and figure out a system that at least *most* people agree on?

□□□□□□□□□□

Let's go back to the idea that right and wrong are just common sense—that, somewhere deep down, we all just *know* good and evil when we see them.

I've already talked about how I think real life is more complicated than that. But still, I don't want to throw this idea out completely. I *do* think we have some kind of deep inner sense of right and wrong (which raises the question, *Where does that deep inner sense come from?*—but more on that later).

But I also think our ability to recognise right and wrong is deeply broken—it's like a busted-up compass that doesn't point north anymore—which means common sense might be *helpful*, but it's not enough all by itself, and here's why.

If you look back through history, you'll find plenty of ideas and beliefs and attitudes that people thought were "common sense" back then, but that seem absolutely awful to us today.

That practice of abandoning unwanted babies that we looked at in the last chapter is one obvious example of this, but we don't have to go all the way back to Ancient Rome to find more.

Not so long ago, it was "common sense" that women shouldn't be allowed to vote.

Not so long ago, it was "common sense" that people should be allowed to own other people as slaves.

This was just how things were—and most people (most of the ones in charge, anyway) didn't even question it.

Good thing we know better now, right?

Most of us look back on those attitudes from the past, and we're horrified—although, the truth is, it's not as simple as that; there are versions of both these attitudes that still cause plenty of harm today. But I'm going to go ahead and assume that you, like me, look back on these attitudes and wonder, "How on earth did they think that was ok?"

But I once heard pastor Timothy Keller make a really interesting point about all this: if *we* look back and cringe at the messed-up ideas about morality that our great-grandparents thought were "common sense"—if we can look back through history and see all the ways *they* got it wrong... then what makes us so sure that, a hundred years from now, our grandchildren and great-grandchildren won't look back at *us* and cringe at *our* ideas about what's right and wrong?

What opinions that we assume are just common sense will future generations look back on with horror and wonder, "How on earth did they think that was ok?"

When we talk about "common sense", all we're really talking about is what seems obvious to most people in our culture at this particular moment.

But if our great-grandparents' common sense let them down in a whole bunch of ways that seem *obvious* to us today, what makes us so sure our common sense won't let us down too?

□ □ □ □ □ □ □ □ □ □

Still, if deciding what's right and wrong together is the best option we've got, we're going to have to figure it out somehow, right?

Maybe future generations *will* look back on us and point out all the ways they think we got it wrong, but don't we have to at least *try*?

You might look back at all those messed-up ideas from the past and say, "Well, at least that proves things are getting better over time!"

But I think there's an even deeper question here: What do we even mean by "better"? Who gets to decide what's better and what's worse?

□ □ □ □ □ □ □ □ □ □

Let's say you meet someone who's decided that, actually, all those people through history who thought slavery was fine and good were right. He's kidnapped a bunch of people and he's making them work in his factory. He says they're his property.

You try to talk him out of it. You tell him slavery is wrong.

He says, "I disagree. I think it's fine."

You point out that he's making his slaves miserable.

He says, "Why shouldn't I make them miserable? This isn't making me miserable. It's making me happy and rich!"

You say they're human beings; they have a right to be happy and free!

He says, "No they don't. Who told you that? There's no such thing as human rights."

You tell him everybody knows human beings have rights.

He says, "That's just their opinion. I have a different opinion. Agree to disagree."

You say it's not about *opinions*. Slavery is just *wrong*.

He just shrugs. "Who says?"

How do you respond to that? Well, hopefully, by calling the authorities and getting him arrested and thrown into prison—but just forcing him to stop doesn't mean you've proven him wrong.

I mean, hopefully you agree with me that he *is* wrong. But again, what do we even mean by "wrong"? Why do *we* get to decide that and not him?

□□□□□□□□□□

Let's take things a step further. Imagine a situation where it's not just this one guy. Imagine society in general starts changing its mind about slavery. What if, little by little, people start to think maybe slavery isn't such a bad idea after all?

Opinions start to change. More and more people decide they'd like to own a few slaves. Eventually, the world decides to put it to a vote: should we move slavery out of the "evil" category and into the "good" category?

The votes are cast and it's a landslide; the people of the world have agreed overwhelmingly to declare that slavery is now a *good* thing.

Now, this might be a ridiculous scenario—but hang in there with me, because here's the big question: if the whole world voted to declare slavery good, would that actually *make* it good?

Before you answer, let's think about what each answer *means*.

If we say *yes*, what we're actually saying is that, when you get right down to it, right and wrong are just opinions—that we just made them up. Sure, murder and prejudice and slavery might be "wrong" *today*, but we could make them "right" tomorrow just by changing our minds about them.

But like I've said already, I don't think anyone really believes this. People might say that right and wrong are just human inventions, but those people still live as if they're more than that. Even if humanity *did* vote slavery back into the "good" category, my guess is that these people would still think it was just as wrong as you do.

On the other hand if we answer *no*—if we agree that we *can't* make murder or slavery or prejudice ok just by changing our minds about them; that these things are just *wrong*, no matter what our opinions might be—then that leads us to a really interesting question:

If right or wrong really do exist, but if we can't just *choose* what they are, even together as a group, then where *do* right and wrong come from?

It seems to me that if right and wrong aren't things we *decide*, then they must be things we *discover*.

So how in the world do we do that?

Chapter 4

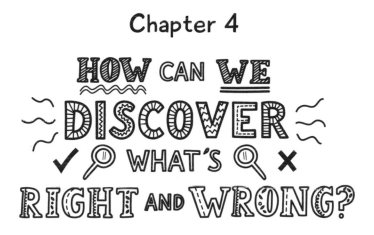

HOW CAN WE DISCOVER ✓ 🔍 WHAT'S 🔍 ✗ RIGHT AND WRONG?

As far as I can see, we've basically got two options. Option 1 is that "right" and "wrong" are really just ideas that human beings have invented for themselves. They might be really *helpful* ideas that keep society running and (sometimes) stop us all from murdering each other—but in the end, they're still just categories we made up. Right and wrong aren't *real* in the same way that gravity is real. They're not unchangeable facts about the universe. They're just ideas we (sometimes) agree on. Which, to me, sounds a whole lot like we're all trying really hard to believe in something that doesn't actually exist.

Option 2 is that right and wrong are bigger than us— that they *are* unchangeable facts about the universe, as true and real as biology and chemistry and physics. Even if every single person in the world agreed that slavery or bullying or murder or abandoning newborn babies on the street was right, it would *still* be wrong, because morality isn't something we just get to invent and reinvent however we choose.

But if my hunch is right that Option 2 is the truth—if right and wrong don't start with us—then where *do* they start? If we don't just get to *decide* what's right and wrong, then how do we *discover* what's right and wrong?

□ □ □ □ □ □ □ □ □ □

I have friends who would tell you that the best way to explain our deep feelings about right and wrong is to look back into the distant past, at the way our species has evolved.

If you're a little fuzzy on the theory of evolution, the idea is that, in nature, the biggest game in town is *survival*. The better suited to your environment you are, the more likely you are to survive long enough to pass your DNA on to the next generation.

What this means is that, over time, a species will develop and change, generally holding onto traits that help it survive and losing traits that make it more likely to get killed or eaten.

When it comes to morality, the idea goes that, way back in the distant past, our ancestors who worked together tended to survive longer and more often than our ancestors who didn't—and so, over the countless generations, that instinct to stick together became deeper and deeper and stronger and stronger. Then, as they developed the ability to speak, our ancestors started sharing more complex information and stories that helped us survive together in groups. Now it wasn't just our DNA that shaped how our species developed and changed; it was our ideas.

Fast-forward to today, and we have these *deep* feelings about right and wrong, but the true *source* of those feelings is our evolutionary history. For the most part, the beliefs and behaviours we call *right* are the ones that, in the past, helped us to survive, while the beliefs and behaviours we call *wrong* are the ones that made us more likely to die.

Now, I'm guessing that readers of this book will have various opinions about evolution as a way of explaining where human beings came from—but whatever your view, let me tell you why I'm not sure this explanation helps us out with the question of morality quite as much as some people think.

□□□□□□□□□□

The first thing to say is that, while science does a great job of helping us understand how things *are*, it has nothing to say about how things *should* be.

In nature, when a group of lions attacks a herd of antelope, the antelope all make a run for it, and the ones that get picked off and eaten tend to be the slowest and weakest— often the very young or the very old.

Now, you might find that *sad*, but no one's suggesting we round up the lions and throw them into prison for hunting antelope; and no one's suggesting we throw the faster, stronger antelope into prison for leaving their family behind either. These animals aren't being *evil*; they're just being animals.

On the other hand, if a strong, powerful country invades and enslaves a weaker, less powerful country...

Or if a fit, strong, healthy mum or dad runs out of a burning building, leaving grandma and the kids inside to take care of themselves...

I mean, we have a problem with that, right?

We say strong nations *shouldn't* use their power to destroy weak nations. We say a fit and healthy parent *should* do what they can to help the vulnerable people in the family.

But why?

We don't blame stronger animals for eating weaker animals, or for leaving them behind to get eaten—and if evolution is the whole story, aren't we just animals too? Isn't the strong surviving and the weak dying absolutely natural and normal? Isn't that just how life works?

You might say, "Yeah, but animals don't know any better. Humans do. We have a responsibility to be good to each other."

But that just brings us back around to the same set of questions: Who are you to say what's "better"? Who are you to say what's "good"? Who are you to say what anyone else is "responsible" for?

I mean, don't get me wrong, I *agree* with you. But we didn't get that from nature. Nature might help explain why we *feel* this way, but that doesn't make it *true*.

If it *is* true, then that truth comes from somewhere else altogether.

□ □ □ □ □ □ □ □ □ □

A while back, at a winter holiday camp my church was running, I invited some kids up to the front of the group for an admittedly-kind-of-weird activity I'd invented called "Is It a Good One?"

The week before, I'd ordered a bunch of mystery items from Amazon: a little bulb-shaped object with a hole through the middle of it; a round, flat rubber thing that looked like it might button up around your neck; a slightly-menacing-looking yellow device with a row of blunt metal slicer-looking bits at one end.

I handed one of these objects to each of my volunteers and asked, "What do you think? Is it a good one?"

And every time, I got the same answer: "How am I supposed to know? I don't know what this thing even is!"

Which made perfect sense, right? Before they could say whether any of these weird bits of plastic was a "good one" or a "bad one", first they needed to know what its *purpose* was—what it was made for. As soon as I filled the kids in on *that*, the rest was easy enough to figure out.

The bulb-shaped thing was a tiny funnel for pouring liquids from one bottle to another—and as it turned out, it was a pretty good one! It did what it was created to do.

Sadly, the flat rubber thing (a hat made to keep sun and rain out of a baby's eyes) and the scary yellow thing (a banana slicer) turned out not to be very good ones at all; when we tried them out they both *failed* to do what they were created to do.

And the whole point of this game (if you can even call it that) was to say that the same basic thing is true about people: before you can figure out whether someone is a "good" person or a "bad" person, first you need to know what a person is *for*—what our *purpose* is. We can't tell whether our actions are "good" or "bad" unless we know what it is that we're *meant* to be doing in the first place. We need to know what a human life is *supposed* to look like before we can see how we measure up.

And this is where, like I said before, I think we need to bring God into it.

Because if evolution is the whole story, if there's no God who made us, if we're all just here by accident, then human beings aren't *for* anything. We're not here for any particular purpose, besides whatever purpose we might invent for ourselves—which means that, in the end, everything we say about what people *should* and *shouldn't* do is really just a matter of opinion.

On the other hand, if there is a God out there—the kind of God the Bible talks about, who has created human beings on purpose and *for* a purpose—then suddenly, we have a solid starting point for figuring out what's right and wrong. We can tell the difference between a "good" person and a "bad" person by asking, "Are they living the way human beings were *created* to live?"

Obviously, none of that *proves* that the God of the Bible (or any other god for that matter) is actually out there—but let's imagine for a moment that he is.

If there really is a God who can help us make sense of right and wrong, what difference might that actually make to us in real life?

Chapter 5

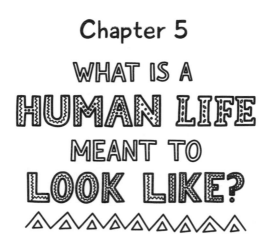

WHAT IS A HUMAN LIFE MEANT TO LOOK LIKE?

There's this famous scene in the Gospel of Matthew, one of the four biographies of Jesus in the Bible, where an expert in the religious law comes up to Jesus and tests him with a question: "Teacher, which is the greatest commandment in the Law?" (Matthew 22 v 36).

In other words, out of everything God has ever taught his people through all of history about who they were meant to be and how they were meant to live, what is the *most* important thing?

Which, really, is just another way of asking the exact same questions we're trying to get to the bottom of: What's the true purpose that human beings have been created for? What does it mean for us to be good rather than evil? If God's the one who truly gets to define right and wrong, then how exactly does he define them?

Well, here's how Jesus answered: "'Love the Lord your God

with all your heart and with all your soul and with all your mind.' This is the first and greatest commandment. And the second is like it: 'Love your neighbour as yourself'" (v 37-39).

What, according to Jesus, is the true purpose of your life? What does it mean for you to be a good person?

Love God, fully and completely.

Love people, fully and completely.

And that's it. If you fully obey those two instructions (which are really just two halves of the *same* instruction), Jesus says you'll be living out the purpose you've been created for (v 40).

Now, at this point, you may be thinking, *Wait. Are you seriously telling me I've read through four whole chapters just for you to tell me that it's good to love people? Thanks so much, but I'm pretty sure I could have figured that out for myself.*

And, sure, that might sound simple enough—but I actually don't think it gets us very far until we figure out exactly what Jesus means by love.

□□□□□□□□□□

See, here's the thing: I love burgers.

I mean, I *really* love them.

And my absolute favourite burgers of all time come from

this amazing place a few minutes from my apartment. Their regular menu is fantastic enough, but what really sets this place apart is their limited-time-only weekly special.

Previous hits have included the Grand Puba (beef patty, bacon jam, provolone cheese, fried onion strings, charred jalapenos, and black garlic aioli), Takeshi's Castle (chicken katsu, braised pork belly, wasabi mayo, togarashi spices, roasted sesame, and Japanese slaw), and maybe the greatest of all, the Fat Elvis (southern fried chicken, streaky bacon, caramelised banana, spicy satay, and mixed berry jam.)

I know, I know: they sound ridiculous. They *are* ridiculous. But they are also incredibly, indescribably, melt-in-your-mouth *delicious*.

From the bottom of my heart, I *love* these burgers.

But what do I actually mean when I say that?

Well, I mean these burgers bring me some temporary happiness; I like how eating them makes me *feel*. And so I take what I want from them until I've had enough, and then I leave whatever's left behind and get on with my life.

When I say, "I love these burgers," what I'm really saying is, "I love what I *get* from these burgers".

Which is all well and good when it comes to burgers—but it's a serious problem when we bring that same attitude into our relationships with God or people.

When you say you love your friends and family, I really hope you mean something different to, "I'll take what I want from you until I've had enough and then I'll leave you behind and get on with my life".

The truth is, "love" means different things to different people in different situations. So what exactly did Jesus mean when he talked about love?

ooooooooo

Well, thankfully, he didn't just talk.

In another one of Jesus' biographies, we get a glimpse at what Jesus was up to in the hours before he was arrested and nailed to a cross.

Jesus' whole life on earth had been leading up to this moment. For months, his enemies had been waiting for a chance to kill him—and at last, the opportunity had arrived. Judas Iscariot, one of Jesus' closest friends, had agreed to sell his teacher out. This time tomorrow, Jesus would be dead and buried.

Jesus had repeatedly warned his followers where things were heading. He told them it *had* to happen this way— that this was all part of God's plan to bring his lost children home to himself. But knowing what was about to happen didn't make it any easier.

So how would Jesus spend his last night with his followers?

In John 13 v 1-4 we read:

> *It was just before the Passover Festival. Jesus knew that the hour had come for him to leave this world and go to the Father. Having loved his own who were in the world, he loved them to the end. The evening meal was in progress, and the devil had already prompted Judas, the son of Simon Iscariot, to betray Jesus. Jesus knew that the Father had put all things under his power, and that he had come from God and was returning to God; so—*

Let me pause right there for a second.

How would you expect that sentence to end?

What the writer is telling us here is that, in this moment, Jesus knew exactly what was about to happen to him—and he knew exactly who he was: the mighty prince of the entire universe, with power and authority over absolutely everything.

And what did Jesus do with all this knowledge and power?

> *Jesus knew that the Father had put all things under his power, and that he had come from God and was returning to God; so—*

So what?

So he ordered his disciples to serve him a meal? So he pulled together an army and overthrew his enemies? So he set himself up on a throne in a palace somewhere?

Nope.

> *Jesus knew that the Father had put all things under his power, and that he had come from God and was returning to God; so he got up from the meal, took off his outer clothing, and wrapped a towel around his waist. After that, he poured water into a basin and began to wash his disciples' feet, drying them with the towel that was wrapped around him. (v 3-5)*

What did Jesus do with all his knowledge and power?

He lowered himself to the place of a servant. He got down on his hands and knees and started scrubbing the dirt from his friends' feet—even the feet of the one he knew was already preparing to betray him.

And notice, John doesn't say that Jesus knew he was God *but* he decided to serve his friends anyway. He's not saying, *Wow! What an ungodlike thing for Jesus to do!*

John says Jesus knew he was God *so* he served his friends. As in, *because* Jesus was God, he served his friends.

What Jesus is showing us here is that this kind of beautiful, undeserved, putting-other-people-first generosity is just *who God is*.

It's not some new thing Jesus was trying out in this moment.

This is exactly who God has *always* been.

This is exactly what his love has *always* looked like.

◻◻◻◻◻◻◻◻◻◻

It can be easy sometimes to imagine God as distant, or uncaring, or even mean—to worry that maybe he doesn't really care all that much about us—but Jesus shows us the truth: that God is love.

And what does that love look like?

It looks like the mighty prince of the entire universe, with power and authority over absolutely everything, crouched on the floor, washing the filth from his friends, making them clean again.

And then Jesus says, *Do this for each other* (v 14-17).

If we want to know what goodness is, *this* is where I think we need to start: with God's perfect, unchanging love—the love that has existed since before the beginning of the universe.

And it's not just that God *decides* what's good, and then tells us; it's that God's perfect love *is* what's perfectly good. The true definition of goodness isn't a set of instructions *from* God; it's *God himself*.

The closer our lives line up with God's own perfect love, the more *good* they are.

The further our lives drift from that love, the less good they are.

According to Jesus, when we know who God is, and when

we know who he made *us* to be, we've discovered the one true solid foundation for figuring out what's right and wrong.

□□□□□□□□□□

But right now, maybe you're thinking, *That all sounds really nice and everything—but that still doesn't prove that what the Bible says is true.*

Ok. Sure. You're right.

For the record, I think there's plenty of great evidence that it is true (and if you want to dig deeper, I've written a whole other book in this series called *How Do We Know that Christianity is Really True?*).

But for now, I want to focus in on a slightly different question: which way of understanding things actually makes the most sense of the world you live in?

Think about it this way. Whatever other thoughts you might have about right and wrong, can we at least agree on a couple of basic ideas?

Can we agree on the idea of equal human rights—that every human being is important and valuable and deserving of dignity and respect?

And can we also agree on the idea of universal kindness— that it's important to be kind to the people around us, even if those people are different from us?

46

Equal human rights and universal kindness.

I mean, those are just the basics, right?

Here's the thing, though.

If you believe Jesus was right—if you believe there's a God of love who calls every human being precious and valuable, who created us to live in loving friendship with him and with each other—then equal human rights and universal kindness make complete logical sense.

If someone asks, "Why should I live like that?" a follower of Jesus can answer, "Of *course* we should treat each other with love and dignity and kindness! That's what we were *created* for!"

On the other hand, if you don't believe there's a God out there—if you believe we're not here for any particular purpose, that we're all just here by accident—and if you *still* say that human beings deserve equal human rights and universal kindness…

Then I think you need to ask yourself, is that the *most* logical conclusion, based on the other things you say you believe?

Does your belief in human rights and universal kindness actually match up with your belief that we're just the random products of a mindless universe?

Aren't equal human rights and universal kindness the complete *opposite* of how you think our species came to exist? So why do we suddenly have to live by those rules now?

If someone asks, "Why should I live like that?" how are you going to answer?

Now, obviously, I'm not saying that only people who follow Jesus can be kind, moral people. That would be ridiculous. But here's what I *am* saying:

If you *know* every human being has equal value and dignity...

If you *know* every human being deserves to be treated with kindness and respect...

If you *know*, somewhere deep down, that those ideas aren't just *opinions*, but that they're *true*...

Then doesn't all that make a whole lot more sense if there's a God out there who *makes* them true?

Chapter 6

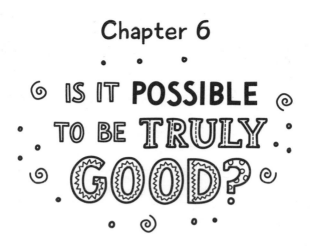

IS IT POSSIBLE TO BE TRULY GOOD?

L et's step back and take a look at where we've been so far.

The world is full of conflicting ideas about what's right and wrong. Sure, it might be easy enough to find a few basic moral ideas we all say we agree on, but that still leaves us with some major issues.

First, even if we can agree on those basic ideas, agreeing on the best way to actually *live out* those ideas is another story. And if, for instance, we agree that we should love one another but we disagree on what loving one another actually *means*, are we really even agreeing after all?

So what do we do? Well, letting everyone create their own *personal* definitions of right and wrong turns out not to be a great solution because, sooner or later, "agree to disagree" just doesn't cut it. We all have some things we believe are *truly* right or wrong, no matter what anyone else says.

But working together to create *shared* definitions of right and wrong falls down too, because even if we *could* somehow manage to get everyone on the same page, that still leaves us with the question, "Who says?"

And to that question, there are really only two answers:

The first answer is, *"We* say". We admit that, in the end, what we call "right" and "wrong" are really just a set of rules we've agreed on together—that nothing is *truly* right or wrong in a way that we can't just go back and change our minds about later. But do you honestly believe that? Does anyone?

The second answer is, *"Someone else* says". This means admitting that morality is bigger than us, that there's some *other* standard of right and wrong that stays the same, whatever our opinions might be.

Which, like I said, is where I think we need to bring God into it—because as far as I can see, the only way to figure out if a person is living rightly or wrongly is to first figure out what a person is *for*.

And while, obviously, there are countless ideas about God out there, I think the Bible's vision of God—the God who has revealed himself most clearly in Jesus—makes sense of our lives, our world, and our deepest instincts about right and wrong in a way that nothing else can.

For one thing, the Bible's vision of God confirms our suspicions that we're here for a purpose. Even those of us who say we believe life has no deep meaning or purpose *still* live as if it does—and the God of the Bible says, *You're absolutely right!* He says you're not just some cosmic accident; you're here on purpose, and you're here *for* a purpose.

And whatever else we might spend our time and energy on, I think most of us have a hunch that the truest, best purpose we could devote our lives to is *love*—and again, the God of the Bible says, *You're absolutely right!* He says that love isn't just a nice idea, it's the whole reason we've been created. Which means the true definition of *right* is *love for God and others*—and the true definition of *wrong* is anything that goes against that.

Of course, like I said, a major part of the trouble is that we can't all agree on what love is supposed to *look* like in an everyday human life—but, in Jesus, God has come to earth in person to show us exactly that. In Jesus, God has given us the most incredible picture of love that the world has ever known.

But that leads us right into our next big problem:

Even with a perfect example to guide us, *knowing* what's right isn't the same thing as *doing* what's right.

Even when the right thing to do seems completely clear to us, why do we still have so much trouble actually *doing* it?

□□□□□□□□□□

On the opening pages of the Bible, we find a story about God's first people that's also a story about what *all* people are like.

It begins with God creating human beings in his image (Genesis 1 v 27), to reflect his perfect love and goodness out into the world, and to partner with him in ruling and caring for his creation (v 28). God gives the first people a home to live in (2 v 8), and in this home, he sets a choice in front of them.

The choice comes in the form of two trees: one with fruit that he welcomes them to eat, because it will lead to life, and another with fruit that he warns them *not* to eat, because it will lead to death (v 17). Which might all seem a bit strange to you, but don't get caught up on the trees, because here's the actual question God's asking them:

Will the first people let him and his perfect love define good and evil—or will they *doubt* his love and come up with their own version of what's right and wrong?

The first people make their choice.

First, they doubt God's love for them. They believe the lie that God isn't good—or at least, not as good as he could be. They imagine that he's holding out on them, holding them back from true happiness—that they'd be better off taking control for themselves.

And so God's first people decide to reinvent good and evil for themselves.

They eat the fruit God told them not to eat (3 v 6). They reject and disobey God. They take what God has called *wrong* and they call it *right*. They take what God has called *right* and they turn their backs on it.

Their failure to trust in God's love becomes a failure to love and obey God the way he deserves—which, as the story goes on, spills over into a failure to love one another.

By turning their backs on God, God's first people cut themselves off from healthy relationship with him, from healthy relationships with each other, and from the full, free, eternal life they were created for. In the end, the penalty for rejecting the God who gives them life is exactly what you'd expect—exactly what he warned them it would be: death.

If the purpose of life is love, then doesn't it make perfect sense that a *failure* to love would be the thing that made it all fall apart?

And that's exactly what we see.

□ □ □ □ □ □ □ □ □ □

But, again, this story isn't just about them.

Remember what I said before about how our ability to recognise right and wrong is deeply broken—how it's like a busted-up compass that doesn't point north anymore?

This is why.

The reason behind all the other reasons we struggle to *know* what's right—and even when we know it, to *do* what's right—is that, deep down, we keep believing the same lie the first people did.

Maybe we doubt that God is even there. Or if he is, we don't believe he really loves us; not as much as he could, anyway. And so we either ignore him or deliberately reject him when he tells us what's *truly* right and wrong. We think we'll be happier if we come up with our own definitions.

And so that's exactly what we do.

But this road always ends in disaster.

Why?

Because God is love.

He's perfectly *loving*, and he's our perfect *standard* of what real love and goodness look like.

Which means "the way God tells us to live" and "the right thing to do" and "what's best for us" and "the way to find true freedom and happiness" aren't four different categories.

They're only ever always *the exact same thing*.

Living the way God tells us to live is the right way to live, which is the best thing for us, which is the way to find true freedom and happiness.

The trouble is, none of us fully believe this. None of us trust in God's perfect love enough to actually live as if it's true—enough to *treat God* as if it's true.

We don't love God and each other—or at least, we don't do it fully and completely, the way Jesus said we were created to do (Matthew 22 v 37-39). And even when we do the right thing on the outside, our motives are often all messed up on the inside.

And so that story about the first people turns out to be a perfect picture of the situation we *all* land ourselves in: cut off from healthy relationship with God, cut off from healthy relationships with each other, and cut off from the full, free, eternal life we were created for.

But the story doesn't end there.

□□□□□□□□□□

They say nobody's perfect—but thankfully, there's an exception.

Jesus was the one person in all of history who completely trusted *and* completely lived out God's true vision of what's right and wrong—the only one who perfectly loved God his Father and everyone else around him.

Jesus is the one truly, perfectly good person.

Which means that if all Jesus came to be was an example for us to follow, that wouldn't actually have helped us very much—because Jesus is *too good!* There's *no way* we could ever measure up to that perfect standard of love.

But Jesus didn't come here to show us how to get it right ourselves; he came because he knew we *couldn't* get it right ourselves.

When Jesus lived that perfect life, he lived it *for us*.

And when Jesus died—when he was arrested and falsely accused and beaten up and murdered on a cross—he did that for us too.

On the cross, Jesus, the one person who *always* got it right, gave up his life to pay for all the ways the rest of us get it wrong. He paid the penalty for all the countless ways we refuse to trust in God's true vision of right and wrong, and for all the damage we cause as we try to reinvent morality without him (Romans 6 v 23; 2 Corinthians 5 v 21). Jesus died so that we could be forgiven.

And then Jesus rose from the dead, proving that he really had opened up the way for us to come back home to God.

Now anyone who puts their trust in Jesus—anyone who turns back to God, admits that they've fallen short of the perfect love he made them for, and asks for his forgiveness—can be welcomed back into friendship with God, not based on their own goodness, but on *Jesus'* goodness (Romans 3 v 21-26; 10 v 9).

Which means that, no matter how badly you've messed up—no matter how often or how completely you've ignored God's vision of right and wrong and tried to reinvent good and evil for yourself—you can *still* come back to Jesus and find forgiveness from the one whose perfect love never runs out.

And as we put our trust in Jesus, God's own Spirit comes to make his home with us, helping us to believe more and more in the truth of his love and goodness. He transforms us day by day into the kind of people who *can* more fully live out God's perfect vision of right and wrong (Romans 5 v 5; John 14 v 26 -27; Ezekiel 36 v 27; Galatians 5 v 24-25)— not to *earn* God's love and acceptance, but out of gratitude to God that, thanks to Jesus, we already have it.

Chapter 7

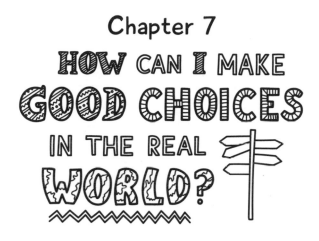

HOW CAN I MAKE GOOD CHOICES IN THE REAL WORLD?

Ok. But what does all this actually look like in real life?

Because so far, we've spent a whole bunch of time talking about where right and wrong come from and who gets to define them—and that's all great and important to wrap our minds around. But none of that makes all that much difference until we put it into practice and start figuring out how to actually live in the real world, right?

We've also mostly been focusing on "right" and "wrong" as separate, black-and-white categories that we can sort our choices into: "Loving people is *right*; murdering people is *wrong*". Which, by now, may have left you wondering, *Isn't real life actually so much more complex than that?*

What do we do in all those situations where the right thing to do isn't obvious—where life feels complicated and confusing and we don't know how to move forward?

What do we do when we're not just deciding between a *good choice* on the one hand and an *evil choice* on the other? What about all the times when we have a whole bunch of different possibilities in front of us that all seem to have their upsides and downsides—when we're not just trying to figure out what's *good*, but what's *best*?

Well, this is where we need to start talking about *wisdom*.

□ □ □ □ □ □ □ □ □ □ □

Let's say you're getting ready to go to the beach. Your friends are coming to pick you up in 15 minutes. And, intelligent person that you are, you already have a bunch of knowledge about your situation:

1. You know that, according to the weather forecast, it's going to be a hot, sunny day today.

2. You know that being out in the sun too long without some kind of protection can lead to sunburn in the short term and increased risk of skin cancer in the long term.

3. You know that you own a hat, sunscreen and a beach umbrella.

Those are the facts. That's the *knowledge* you have. And all those things are good and interesting to know.

But none of that is *wisdom*. Wisdom is the next step: not just knowing the right information, but taking what you know and using it to make good choices in the real world.

Which, in this case, means wearing your hat and putting on some sunscreen every few hours and putting up your umbrella to shade you from the sun.

Wisdom is not just being smart—because you can be really, really smart and still make really, really terrible choices. Wisdom is taking what you know and putting it to work.

□□□□□□□□□□

So far, so obvious.

I mean, deciding to wear a hat on a hot day *does* take wisdom—but not much of it. There's a pretty obvious wise choice and a pretty obvious not-so-wise choice.

Ok. What about this one?

Two of your friends have gotten into an argument and now they aren't speaking to each other. Do you stand back and let them sort it out between the two of them? Or do you step in and try to help them figure it out?

That's harder, right?

Because there's no one-size-fits-all rule. *Sometimes* the most helpful thing is to step in and give your advice—but *sometimes* the most helpful thing is to just stay out of it.

So how do you choose? What's the right answer?

Well, it depends on the situation.

And this is where wisdom is particularly necessary and valuable—in all the times where the right thing to do depends on the situation.

In this case, wisdom means asking questions like:

"Do my friends actually need help, or can they work this fight out on their own?"

"Do I really think I can help here, or do I actually just kind of enjoy the drama?"

"Am I really the best person to help, or is there someone else I should rope in?"

"If I do get involved, what am I going to say?"

"How can I avoid taking sides and do what's best for both people in this situation?"

And those answers are going to be different in each situation.

That's what makes wisdom so tricky—but it's also why it's so necessary.

We need wisdom to use what we know to make good choices in the real world, where things are messy and there's not always a simple answer.

▫▫▫▫▫▫▫▫▫▫

So if wisdom really is as important and valuable as the Bible says it is, how do you get it?

Well, here's some more helpful advice from Timothy Keller: "Wisdom is a pathway, not a door".

How do you get through a door? You do it all at once. Open the door. Step through. Done.

But a path is different. You don't get down a path all at once; you get there one step at a time.

And that's what wisdom is like. Unfortunately, there's no magic shortcut. You don't find wisdom all at once. You get it a step at a time, a day at a time, a choice at a time.

If you're faced with a tough decision and you make what turns out to be a good choice—great! Learn from it, and keep going.

On the other hand, if you make what turns out to be a terrible choice—well, that's unfortunate. But pick yourself up, learn from it, and keep going.

Every choice you make is an opportunity to grow in wisdom.

ooooooooooo

Now, I said there's no magic shortcut down the path of wisdom—and that's true. But the good news is, we have something far better than a shortcut; we have a guide:

Trust in the Lord *with all your heart and lean not on your own understanding; in all your ways submit to him, and he will make your paths straight. (Proverbs 3 v 5-6)*

In other words, if you want to continue down the path of wisdom, you *could* just do that by trial and error—by trying to figure it out all on your own. Or you could ask the people around you for advice, which, depending on who you choose to ask, might work out pretty well for you—or not. But if you *really* want to grow in wisdom, surely the best place to go is straight to the source.

Because wisdom is about how we use what we know—and, sure, we know some stuff, but God knows everything.

Wisdom is about making the best possible choices in the real world—and, sure, we've spent a bunch of time in the real world, but God *made* the real world, and he knows it inside out; he knows the best possible way forward in every possible situation.

Wisdom is a path—and, sure, we're somewhere on that path; hopefully, we're further along that path today than we were a month or a year or five years ago. But just like God's love shows us true *goodness*, it also shows us true *wisdom*.

In the end perfect wisdom is just perfect love, lived out in real life—and so by far the best way to keep growing in wisdom is to keep getting to know Jesus, the one person who perfectly embodied God's love in a human life.

So here's my advice: read and re-read the biographies of Jesus in the Bible, connect with Jesus through prayer, and get hooked in with a community of Jesus' followers who can share what they've already learned with you.

And as you move through life, and as you face complicated moral decisions where there's no clear-cut right-or-wrong answer, pray for God's guidance, and run those decisions through the same simple grid Jesus used:

Am I loving God and other people?

Am I treating people the way I'd want them to treat me?

And sometimes your answer will be, *I don't know.*

And that's ok too.

Because wisdom is a pathway, not a door. You're not going to get it all at once.

But the more you get to know Jesus, the more you trust in his perfect wisdom instead of trying to work it out all on your own, the more you'll see him straightening out that path in front of you, showing you the right way to go.

Chapter 8

WHAT SHOULD I DO WHEN MY friends DISAGREE WITH ME?

Let's say you become convinced that Jesus' vision of right and wrong really is the best way to live. Let's say you decide to quit trying to define morality for yourself and start letting God's perfect love be the definition of *good* that you live by.

How should you respond to people who disagree with you?

Because, obviously, there will be plenty of situations where people who *don't* follow Jesus will disagree strongly with people who *do* follow Jesus about what's right and wrong—and in particular, about how to *live out* what's right and wrong.

I mean, that's exactly what you'd expect, right?

The Christian vision of right and wrong starts with believing that there's a beginningless, endless God of love who created us for loving friendship with him and each other—and that, in Jesus, that same God has come to earth and shown us what it looks like to perfectly live out that love.

If you believe all that, then the logical response is to follow Jesus' teachings, and to live the way Jesus lived.

But if you *don't* believe it, if you think Jesus was just a good teacher or whatever, then, sure, you might choose to run with a few of his teachings that seem wise to you—but why would anyone expect you to do anything more than that?

So, for example, Jesus tells his followers:

> But I say, love your enemies! Pray for those who persecute you! In that way, you will be acting as true children of your Father in heaven. For he gives his sunlight to both the evil and the good, and he sends rain on the just and the unjust alike.
>
> *(Matthew 5 v 44-45, NLT)*

Being a follower of Jesus means believing that God loves *his* enemies—and, more specifically, that Jesus died to rescue *you* while you were still behaving like an enemy to him. And so the *only* right response to that belief is to treat *your* enemies in the same way—to love them, and to pray for them, and to ask God to be as generous to them as he's been to you.

But if you're *not* a follower of Jesus, if you *don't* believe he's done that, then it's pretty understandable if you think *commanding* people to love their enemies is a bit much. I mean, you *could* try to love your enemies, and it would be really nice if you did—but is it really something people *should* do, whether they want to or not? Suddenly, that doesn't seem so clear.

The Bible is *full* of wisdom about right and wrong that makes *perfect sense* if you believe that God has designed human beings to live in specific ways for specific purposes, but which seems pretty upside-down if you *don't* believe that.

And just telling people they should live the same way as you because "God says" or "the Bible says" isn't going to get you very far—because why would that make any difference to someone who doesn't agree that God or the Bible has any authority over them?

As followers of Jesus, it shouldn't surprise us that we run into disagreement. The question is, what should we do about it?

□ □ □ □ □ □ □ □ □ □

The first thing to keep in mind is that it's not our job to judge our friends who don't yet follow Jesus, or to try to force them to change their behaviour.

There's this letter in the Bible where an early follower of Jesus named Paul is laying out a whole bunch of instructions to one of the first churches about how they should be living. But then he stops to clear something up: he's not telling people *outside* the church what to do;

that's none of his business. The church's responsibility is to focus on what's happening *inside* the church—to make sure *they're* living the way Jesus calls them to live—not to judge anyone else's behaviour; that's God's job (1 Corinthians 5 v 9-13).

Think about it: becoming a follower of Jesus in the first place means admitting that my own behaviour doesn't measure up, that I'm not good enough on my own, but that in his grace and kindness, God treats me infinitely better than I deserve (Romans 3 v 23-24). If that's what I believe, then how in the world could I possibly think I have the right to judge someone else?

Meanwhile, in *any* interaction I have with people who disagree with me, it's so important to remember that even if I'm right about Jesus (and I'm convinced that I am), that doesn't mean I'm right about everything else. We're all still on that path towards wisdom—and we all still have a long way to go. Which means that, chances are, in any conversation we *both* have something to learn from one another.

I'm not saying we shouldn't talk to our friends about what we believe, or why we live the way we do; the Bible says that we should *always* be prepared to gently, respectfully give an answer to anyone who asks us about the hope that we have (1 Peter 3 v 15).

I'm also not saying, when we're sharing our opinion or when our friends ask us for advice, that we shouldn't bring our faith into it; if we believe that the way of Jesus really is the best way to live, then of *course* we'll want to point our friends in that direction!

But our greatest hope and prayer for our friends who don't know Jesus yet shouldn't be that they'd start *behaving* more like Christians; it should be that they come to know Jesus as their rescuer and King!

In the meantime, my job isn't to judge or change the people around me who don't know Jesus yet. It's to love and serve and welcome them, to treat them with kindness, to keep sharing the great news of the hope I have in Jesus—and above all, to *pray* for them, that they would come to know Jesus' love and grace and mercy too.

And whenever *that* happens, *then* we can start using "God says" or "the Bible says" as our way to figure things out together. Until then, we need to recognise and respect the fact that there are plenty of issues we're just not going to agree on, because we're coming to those issues from such different starting points.

□□□□□□□□□□

Ok. But what about all that stuff I was saying before about how we *can't* just agree to disagree about everything? If you're a follower of Jesus, what are you meant to do when you look out at the world and see individual people or your community or even your government calling things "right" that you're convinced Jesus would call "wrong"?

Well, your first option is to get all bitter and judgmental about it—but, as I've just said, I think that attitude really misses the mark (and probably won't get you anywhere anyway).

Another option is to advocate for change: to protest against what you believe is wrong, to write to government leaders, to vote when you're old enough. And there's an important place for all that—as long as we remember that, as followers of Jesus, our job isn't to stand up for our *own* rights, but to look for opportunities to bless and care for others (1 Corinthians 10 v 24; Philippians 2 v 4; Galatians 6 v 10).

It's *right* to feel upset, even angry, about the world's injustice and cruelty and brokenness—that stuff upsets Jesus too! But we need to be careful that our anger doesn't lead us to bring more brokenness into the world (Ephesians 4 v 26). Instead, God calls us to find ways to work for justice and mercy (Micah 6 v 8), and to stand up for the people who can't stand up for themselves (Proverbs 31 v 8-9).

I really like the author Andy Stanley's advice here: "Do for one what you wish you could do for everyone".

You might not be able to solve the whole world's problems—but you can help out with someone's problems. You can be kind to someone who really needs a friend. You can sponsor a child living in poverty. You can look for ways to serve people in need in your neighbourhood.

And above and beyond everything else, following Jesus means never forgetting who's really in charge.

Whatever humans happen to be running things where you live—no matter how good or bad they might be—there's a King in heaven who's infinitely stronger and wiser and more loving and powerful than any of them, and there's no power in all the universe that can stand against his good plans to rescue his children and restore his broken world (Romans 8 v 38-39).

When human leaders or societies work *for* God's will to love and bless the world—to feed the poor, heal the sick, bring justice to the oppressed—then that's beautiful and good and we should celebrate it!

But even when human leaders or societies work *against* God's vision of right and wrong, that still can't derail his plans; he just takes what people mean for evil and uses it for good (Genesis 50 v 20). This doesn't mean those evil acts aren't evil; it doesn't mean we shouldn't try to stop them whenever and wherever we can. What it *does* mean is that evil is not, and never will be, the end of the story.

We see this at the cross, where the ultimate act of human evil—the murder of Jesus himself—became the way God *defeated* the powers of evil; and we can trust that God is still working this way today, even when the pain of life makes that hard to see (Romans 8 v 28).

And I think this means a couple of things for us.

First, it means we don't need to stress out when we face disagreement, either from individuals or from our society in general.

And second, it means we have something far better to do than argue or complain about what's wrong with the world—and that's to bring our hopes and fears and requests to God, to pray for our leaders, and for the people they lead, trusting that God is the one who's ultimately in charge (1 Timothy 2 v 1-4; Romans 13 v 1-5).

oooooooooo

Here's something else that has taken me a long time to learn, but that I'm convinced is true:

If I'm debating just to win the argument, I've already lost.

If I care more about proving that I'm right than I care about loving the person in front of me, I've failed at the thing that matters most—because people are so much more important than arguments.

I'm not saying the truth doesn't matter; of course it does. And I'm convinced Jesus was right when he said he himself is the truth (John 14 v 6).

But as one of the writers of the Bible put it, "If I … can fathom all mysteries and all knowledge, and if I have a faith that can move mountains, but do not have love, I am nothing" (1 Corinthians 13 v 2).

As a follower of Jesus, my main job isn't to show the world how right I am.

It's to love the person in front of me.

It's to keep living, day by day, with the quiet, humble confidence that the way of Jesus really is the best way to live; it's to keep learning to trust more and more deeply in God's unfailing love; and it's to keep doing my best, with the help of God's Holy Spirit, to live in a way that *demonstrates* God's love to everyone around me.

And as I do all that, I'm convinced that the same kind, patient, generous God who brought me home to himself will be working through my life, and my prayers, to do the same for others.

Chapter 9

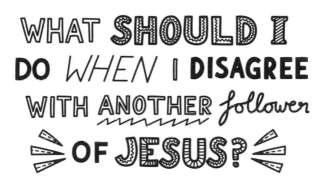

WHAT SHOULD I DO WHEN I DISAGREE WITH ANOTHER follower OF JESUS?

If you've been following Jesus for a while now, or if you've spent much time with people who do, you've probably noticed that followers of Jesus are pretty good at disagreeing with each other.

Sometimes that's Christians arguing on the internet. Sometimes it's one church disagreeing with another church about what the Bible teaches. Sometimes it's people in the *same* church community who can't see eye to eye. Or maybe you've just noticed that, even if you and the other people in your family all follow Jesus, that hasn't magically brought an end to all your arguments.

Turns out, even when you all agree that God is the one who defines what's right and wrong, that doesn't mean you all automatically agree on how exactly that all works out in the real world.

The reasons for this are mostly pretty obvious.

For one thing, we're all still works in progress.

See, the good news is that, since I've put my trust in Jesus, God has forgiven me for all the selfish motives that make it harder for me to *know* what's right and to *do* what's right—stuff like wanting people to think I'm right all the time, or wanting to impress people, or just wanting to have things my own way.

But the bad news is, those old habits are still kicking around inside my heart. Now, I trust that as I follow Jesus, God's Spirit is changing me, day by day, to become more like him—but that's a lifelong process and, in the meantime, my motives are still a bit of a mixed bag. There are plenty of times where what I call "right" still has more to do with what I want than what *God* wants.

And the same is true for every follower of Jesus.

And even putting all that aside for a moment, we're still left with the reality we've been dealing with all along: that even if our basic *ideals* about right and wrong are pretty simple, putting those ideals into practice is often really complicated.

So what should Christians do when they disagree with each other about what's right or wrong?

□ □ □ □ □ □ □ □ □ □

Let's start where all followers of Jesus (hopefully) agree: that figuring out what's right or wrong in any situation means figuring out what *God* has to say. Whatever *our* opinions might be, step one for Jesus' followers is letting God speak.

And while God can speak to us in dreams or visions or a voice we can actually hear or however else he wants, our clearest way of figuring out what God has to say—and the one we can all look at together—is the Bible. As an early follower of Jesus named Paul wrote to his friend Timothy:

> *All Scripture is inspired by God and is useful to teach us what is true and to make us realise what is wrong in our lives. It corrects us when we are wrong and teaches us to do what is right. God uses it to prepare and equip his people to do every good work.*
>
> *(2 Timothy 3:16-17, NLT)*

In the Bible, we find God's timeless, unchanging truth for all people, all over the world, through all of history—which, as followers of Jesus, should be far more important than anything *we* have to say. And so figuring out God's view of right and wrong means coming back, again and again, to the Bible, and letting God use that to shape our lives and our decisions.

□□□□□□□□□

Ok. But in case you haven't noticed, the Bible is kind of a difficult book.

For one thing, the Bible was written down by people living in a completely different time and culture and language to our own, and so before we can figure out what it means for *us*, here and now, first we need to figure out what it meant to its *original* readers, way back then—and that takes a lot of work and wisdom.

And for another thing, the Bible isn't mostly a list of rules or a handy step-by-step guide to living a moral life; it's a big, beautiful, complex, artfully-structured, history-spanning *story*, packed with profound insights that are meant to be discovered and rediscovered over our whole *lifetime*. When two of your friends are fighting, you can't just flip to the *What To Do When Your Friends Are Fighting* section and read out the answer. Again, we need wisdom.

Thankfully, God is ready and willing to help us out. As Jesus' brother James said:

> *If any of you lacks wisdom, you should ask God, who gives generously to all without finding fault, and it will be given to you. (James 1 v 5)*

And so another thing we need to keep on doing whenever we're in a disagreement with another follower of Jesus is *pray*. We should pray that God would help us to keep loving one another well even while we disagree; we should pray that he'd be helping us to hear one another clearly; and we should pray for God's wisdom as we search for an answer, trusting that he's promised to give it to us.

But remember, wisdom is a pathway, not a door. We don't

get it all at once. We *grow* in wisdom, a step at a time. And for as long as we're still on that path, there are going to be times where we keep facing disagreement.

And so what do we do when we've searched the Bible and prayed and talked it all through with one another and we *still* can't agree on what we think God wants us to do?

□ □ □ □ □ □ □ □ □ □

Thankfully, God (and the writers of the Bible) saw this coming, and so the Bible is packed with teaching on what to do even when you *can't* agree. And, as I hope you already suspect by now, it all comes down to love.

Here's Paul again:

> *Do nothing out of selfish ambition or vain conceit. Rather, in humility value others above yourselves, not looking to your own interests but each of you to the interests of the others. In your relationships with one another, have the same mindset as Christ Jesus.*
> *(Philippians 2 v 3-5)*

In other words, any time you're faced with a choice between doing what's best for you and doing what's best for the *other person*, loving like Jesus looks like putting their needs ahead of your own.

This doesn't mean letting people hurt you or take advantage of you. In situations like that, you need to get help or get out—or both.

It also doesn't mean we take something God has called *wrong* and pretend it's ok for the sake of being kind to others—because remember, *what God calls right* and *what's best for us* are only ever the exact same thing; in the end, the best way to be kind to someone is to point them *towards* God's vision of right and wrong, not away from it.

What it *does* mean is that Jesus calls us to show the same love to one another that he's shown to us. And so if you've done everything you can, and you *still* can't come to an agreement, then whatever else you do, just keep on choosing love.

Of course, none of us are going to get this right all the time. But the more we focus our attention on Jesus, the more we keep filling up on *his* love for us, the more energy and confidence we'll have to keep on loving the people around us, trusting that the great God of all love and truth and goodness is right there with us, every step of the way.

Chapter 10

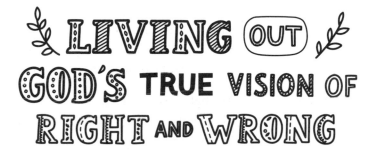

LIVING (OUT) GOD'S TRUE VISION OF RIGHT AND WRONG

Surprisingly often, I find myself deep in conversation with the students at my school about right and wrong and how we're meant to live in the world—and almost always, at some point in the discussion, someone will jump in with these words:

"Nobody's perfect."

And, on one level, I love that expression.

It's a way of naming the truth we all feel that this stuff is *hard*—that, as we've seen all through this book, even in situations where morality seems simple, actually living a good life in a complicated world is, well, *complicated*.

And so when one of my classes and I have found ourselves deep in the weeds of some complex moral issue and someone's put their hand up to remind us that nobody's perfect, I've mostly just nodded in agreement—or maybe reminded them how good it is that Jesus is the exception to that rule—and then moved on.

But recently, I've settled on a different response, one that I think is actually a whole lot more helpful.

"Nobody's perfect."

"Well, not yet, anyway."

ooooooooooo

There's this bit in Mark's biography of Jesus in the Bible where someone calls Jesus "good teacher" and Jesus replies, "Why do you call me good? ... No one is good—except God alone" (Mark 10 v 17-18).

Jesus isn't denying his goodness *or* his God-ness here. He's just pointing to the same reality that my students keep pointing to: that, besides God himself, nobody's perfect. That all of us fall far short of God's perfect standard of love and goodness. That we need God's grace to pull us out of that mess and bring us back into friendship with him (Romans 3 v 23-24).

But the good news of Jesus doesn't end with forgiveness—as extraordinary as that forgiveness is.

Way back in the Old Testament book of Ezekiel, we find this incredible promise from God to his people:

I will give you a new heart and put a new spirit in you; I will remove from you your heart of stone and give you a heart of flesh. And I will put my Spirit in you and move

you to follow my decrees and be careful to keep my laws.
(Ezekiel 36 v 26-27)

In the Bible, talking about our "heart" is a way of talking about what we trust, what we value, what we love.

God says, when you trace the problem all the way back, the reason behind all the other reasons we fall short of God's perfect goodness is that our hearts fail to fully trust in his love for us—and so we reject his definition of good and evil and start making up our own definitions.

But here we see God promising to give his people *new* hearts that do trust in his love for us, so that we *can* fully trust and obey him. (To be clear, this is a metaphor; you are not about to be wheeled in for a surgical procedure.)

This heart change begins the moment we put our trust in Jesus—but when Jesus returns, as he's promised, to redeem and restore our broken world, he'll make that transformation complete.

When Jesus returns, the whole universe will be filled to the brim with his perfect goodness—and if you're putting your trust in him, then *so will you.* Your heart will be so transformed *by* his love, and so convinced *of* his love, that living a life of perfect goodness will be as natural to you as breathing.

This is where the whole story is heading.

In the meantime, the invitation of Jesus is to follow him into the best life possible, here and now, today (John

10 v 10)—to keep getting to know him, to keep modelling your imperfect life as best you can around his perfect one, and to keep trusting that God's Spirit is working in you, moment by moment, to transform your heart (Galatians 4 v 19).

Because, sure, nobody's perfect.

But that's only because this story isn't finished yet.

References

As with all the other titles in this series, the only way I've been able to write this book is by drawing on the work of a whole bunch of other writers and thinkers who know way more about this stuff than I do.

Jon Tyson mentions the historic practice of infant exposure in his book *The Intentional Father*. As I dug deeper into the practice, the most helpful summary I found was in an ABC article by Louise Gosbell entitled, "'As long as it's healthy': What can we learn from early Christianity's resistance to infanticide and exposure?"

The idea that an atheistic view of human evolution leads logically to the conclusion that "right" and "wrong" are really just made-up stories we tell each other is laid out by Yuval Noah Harari in his book, *Sapiens*.

I first encountered the idea that you can't tell whether someone is a good person or a bad person until you figure out what a person is for in Timothy Keller's book, *Making Sense of God*, which was in turn drawing on arguments presented in Alasdair MacIntyre's book, *After Virtue*.

Keller was also my source for the insight that, while we don't cast moral judgement when a stronger animal kills a weaker animal, we *do* cast moral judgement when a stronger country invades a weaker country.

The bit in Chapter 5 about love for food versus love for God and people was inspired by Bible Project's "Agape" video on YouTube. Jon Collins and Tim Mackie at Bible Project are also the ones who gave me the language of "redefining good and evil for themselves" to describe what God's first people were doing when they ate the fruit God told them not to eat.

The idea that equal rights and universal human kindness are the core moral convictions of our secular society comes from Charles Taylor's writing—but, yet again, I have Timothy Keller to thank for bringing that work to my attention. In the "Faith and Proof" episode of his Questioning Christianity podcast, Keller takes Taylor's ideas and makes the case I've gone on to borrow for this book: that these moral convictions make far more logical sense if God exists. (Glen Scrivener's excellent book, *The Air We Breathe*, was also extremely helpful in clarifying my ideas as I edited this section of this book.)

Thank yous

Thanks, as always, to Rachel Jones for being such an insightful and patient editor, to André Parker and Emma Randall for your amazing design work, and to the whole team at TGBC for getting behind this series and helping it to be the best it can be.

Thanks to the staff, students and families of PLC Sydney. It is one of the great privileges of my life to share the good news of Jesus with you every week.

Thanks to Mum and Dad for the countless hours you've poured into talking through my big questions about God over the past 30+ years.

Thanks to Katie and Waz, Phil and Meredith, and Kerryn and Andrew, for your constant love, support, wisdom, and encouragement.

Thanks to Hattie, Liam and Alec, for helping me see the love of God more clearly. May you grow up full of big questions, and may you keep turning back to our great King Jesus for the answers.

Chris Morphew

Thanks to Stephen Brewer for sharpening my thinking (and, hopefully, writing) about evolution.

Thanks to Tom French for being a brilliant writing and podcasting buddy.

Thanks to Rowan McAuley for your endless support and friendship. Let's write another book together soon!

Last but not least, thanks to my church family at Abbotsford Presbyterian. In particular, a huge shout-out to the whole crew at YCentral—may this book help you to see even more clearly the abundant love God has for you in Jesus.

Keep asking big questions:

△ △△△ △△ △△ △

Big Questions is a series of fun and fast-paced books walking you through what the Bible says about some of the big questions of life, helping you to grow in confident and considered faith.

 thegoodbook.co.uk/big-questions
thegoodbook.com/big-questions
thegoodbook.com.au/big-questions

Also by Chris Morphew

A 100-day devotional journey through Mark's fast-paced, action-packed story—bringing you face to face with Jesus: the one who changes everything.

thegoodbook.co.uk/best-news-ever
thegoodbook.com/best-news-ever
thegoodbook.com.au/best-news-ever

COMPANY

BIBLICAL | RELEVANT | ACCESSIBLE

At The Good Book Company, we are dedicated to helping Christians and local churches grow. We believe that God's growth process always starts with hearing clearly what he has said to us through his timeless word—the Bible.

Ever since we opened our doors in 1991, we have been striving to produce Bible-based resources that bring glory to God. We have grown to become an international provider of user-friendly resources to the Christian community, with believers of all backgrounds and denominations using our books, Bible studies, devotionals, evangelistic resources, and DVD-based courses.

We want to equip ordinary Christians to live for Christ day by day, and churches to grow in their knowledge of God, their love for one another, and the effectiveness of their outreach.

Call us for a discussion of your needs or visit one of our local websites for more information on the resources and services we provide.

Your friends at The Good Book Company

thegoodbook.com | thegoodbook.co.uk
thegoodbook.com.au | thegoodbook.co.nz
thegoodbook.co.in